FUNNY RIDDLES
COLORING BOOK

Edited b

Vi

N

Dover Publications, Inc., *New York*

f

Copyright © 1989 by Dover Publications, Inc.
All rights reserved under Pan American and
International Copyright Conventions.

Funny Riddles Coloring Book is a new work,
first published by Dover Publications, Inc., in 1989.

International Standard Book Number: 0-486-26114-X

Manufactured in the United States of America
Dover Publications, Inc.
31 East 2nd Street
Mineola, N.Y. 11501

NOTE

How many funny riddles do you know?
This coloring book contains a total of
sixty—enough to keep you and every-
one around you laughing for a long
time! It's small enough to carry anywhere, so you can read the riddles—
and show the pictures that go with
them—to all your friends. Encourage
them to guess the answers, which are
printed upside down at the bottoms of
the pages. Even if your friends already
know some of the answers, they'll still
enjoy the zany pictures, and might
even want to help you color them!

How are an old car and
a baby alike?

They both have a rattle.

4

What is the best way to
catch a squirrel?

Act like a nut and he'll follow you
anywhere.

What did the big
firecracker say
to the little
firecracker?

"My pop's bigger than your pop!"

6

Why must a doctor always keep his temper?

He can't afford to lose his patients.

Why did the silly billy tiptoe past the medicine chest?

He didn't want to wake the sleeping pills.

Why did the
silly billy
take an axe
to a banana?

He wanted to make a banana split.

I have a head
and a tail
but no body.
What am I?

A penny.

10

What is the tallest building in every city?

The library—it has the most stories.

Why should you never tell
a secret to a pig?

Because he is a squealer.

What happens to ducks when you tell them too many jokes?

They quack up.

Why did the turtle cross the road?

It was the chicken's day off.

14

What do you get when you cross an insect with a rabbit?

Bugs Bunny.

What makes more
noise than a
squawking
parrot?

Two squawking parrots.

Where was the Declaration
of Independence signed?

At the bottom.

Why did the taxi cab driver
go out of business?

He drove all his customers away.

Why did the
schoolteacher
hit the clock?

The clock struck first.

What is the difference
between a skunk and
a bottle of perfume?

If you don't know, then please don't
ever buy me perfume!

How is a party like
a tennis game?

There is always a racket.

What kind of shoes can you make from banana peels?

Slippers.

What did the
tall chimney
say to the
short chimney?

"You're not big enough to smoke!"

Where does a lamb go
for a haircut?

To the baa-baa shop.

What are the
biggest kind
of ants?

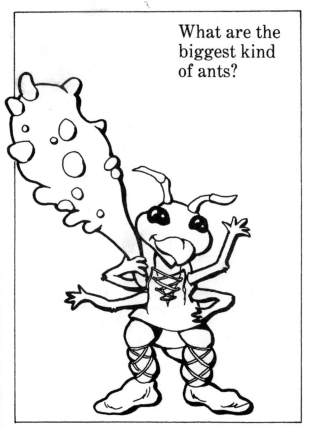

Gi-ants.

What has two heads, four ears, six feet and a tail?

A man on horseback.

What has four wheels
and flies?

A garbage truck.

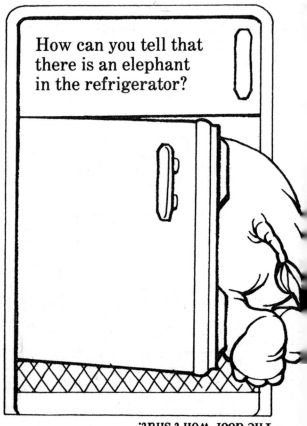

How can you tell that there is an elephant in the refrigerator?

The door won't shut.

28

When do French poodles
have eight legs?

When there are two of them.

Why did the silly billy
throw the stick of butter
out the window?

He wanted to see a butterfly.

What is worse than
finding a worm
in an apple?

Finding half a worm.

What can run
and whistle
but cannot
walk or talk?

A railroad engine.

What did the
boy centipede
say to the
girl centipede?

"You sure have a nice pair of legs,
pair of legs, pair of legs . . ."

Why did the baker get put in jail?

He was always beating up the eggs.

An elephant is sleeping in your bed. What time is it?

Time to get a new bed.

What do you get when you
cross an elephant
with a ghost?

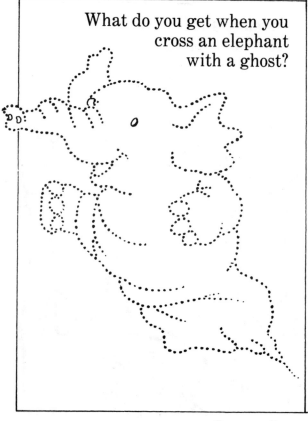

A big nothing.

When is the best time
to milk a cow?

When she is in the moo-d.

What is brown, has a hump and lives at the North Pole?

A lost camel.

What could you call
a sleeping bull?

A bulldozer.

How does a monster count
to fourteen?

On his fingers.

What do you get when
you cross a lemon
with a cat?

A sour-puss.

What do elephants have that no other animals have?

Baby elephants.

42

What did the hen say when she laid a square egg?

"Ouch!"

Why are cherry trees sad?

They are always getting picked on.

If you found an
egg floating in the
Mississippi River,
where would it
have come from?

A hen.

How does a baby ghost cry?

"Boo-hoo! Boo-hoo!"

Where was George Washington when the lights went out?

In the dark.

What insect would
make the best
baseball
player?

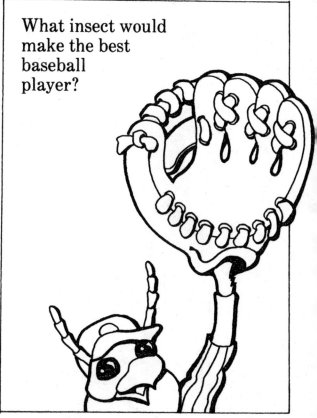

The spider—it always catches flies.

Eleven crows sat
on a scarecrow.
A hunter shot one down.
How many were left?

None. The rest naturally flew away as
soon as they heard the shot.

How do you know that
peanuts are fattening?

Have you ever seen a skinny elephant?

What is the difference
between an old penny
and a new nickel?

Four cents.

How many monkeys can
you put into an
empty barrel?

One. After that, the barrel isn't empty.

What animal can jump higher than a kite?

Any animal. Kites can't jump.

What will happen to
a yellow shell if
you throw it into
the Red Sea?

It will get wet.

Why do birds
fly south
for the winter?

Because it's too far to walk.

What kind of fireman
wears the largest boots?

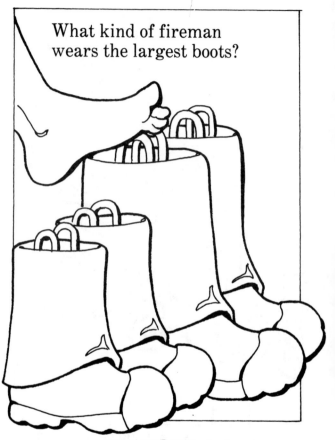

The one with the largest feet.

What did the bedspread
say to the bed?

"Don't move! I've got you covered!"

Why are fishermen the best letter writers?

They are always dropping a line.

What did one candle
say to the other?

"Wanna go out with me tonight?"

What is a pony
after it is
five months old?

Six months old.

What has many teeth but
never has cavities?

A comb.

What bird is with you
at every meal?

The swallow.

When did the
tomato blush?

When it saw the salad dressing.